YO-CAV-595

Workbook to Accompany Future Work

Joseph F. Coates
Jennifer Jarratt
John B. Mahaffie

Workbook to Accompany
FUTURE WORK

Seven Critical Forces
Reshaping Work
and the Work Force
in North America

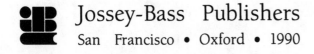

Jossey-Bass Publishers
San Francisco • Oxford • 1990

WORKBOOK TO ACCOMPANY FUTURE WORK
Seven Critical Forces Reshaping Work and the Work Force in North America
by Joseph F. Coates, Jennifer Jarratt, and John B. Mahaffie

Copyright © 1990 by: Jossey-Bass Inc., Publishers
350 Sansome Street
San Francisco, California 94104
&
Jossey-Bass Limited
Headington Hill Hall
Oxford OX3 0BW

Library of Congress Cataloging-in-Publication Data

Coates, Joseph F., date.
    Future work: seven critical forces reshaping work and the work
force in North America/Joseph F. Coates, Jennifer Jarratt, and
John B. Mahaffie. – 1st ed.
        p. cm. – (The Jossey-Bass management series)
    (The Jossey-Bass public administration series)
    (The Jossey-Bass nonprofit sector series)
    Includes bibliographical references.
    ISBN 1-55542-240-3 (alk. paper)
    ISBN 1-55542-246-2 (workbook: alk. paper)
    1. Manpower planning–United States. I. Jarratt, Jennifer.
II. Mahaffie, John B. III. Title. IV. Series.
V. Series: The Jossey-Bass public administration series.
VI. Series: The Jossey-Bass nonprofit sector series.
HF5549.5.M3C63 1990
331.1'0973–dc20   90-35170
                                                   CIP

Manufactured in the United States of America

The paper in this book meets the guidelines for
permanence and durability of the Committee on
Production Guidelines for Book Longevity of the
Council on Library Resources.

JACKET DESIGN BY WILLI BAUM

FIRST EDITION

Code 9052

A joint publication in
The Jossey-Bass Management Series
The Jossey-Bass Public Administration Series
and
The Jossey-Bass Nonprofit Sector Series

CONTENTS

PREFACE

This workbook is designed to accompany *Future Work*. The exercises reinforce the information and trends identified in the book and will help to focus the user's attention on the implications of those trends for his or her own organization. This workbook will do the following things:

- Help the user to know more about the organization and work force familiar to him or her
- Help the user to understand and interpret trends shaping the future of the work force and the range of implications of those trends
- Lead the user to more effective human resources plans and actions in his or her own organization
- Lead the user to proactive planning for the work force over the next ten to fifteen years
- Guide the user in relating trends to the company's or organization's business.

Several assumptions about the users shape the design of this workbook. Users are assumed to fall into the following categories:

- Human resources professionals, operations managers, staff persons, or senior executives concerned with their own companies, organizations, or agencies (in this workbook we use the terms *corporation*, *organization*, and *company* interchangeably, and the user may assume that each question pertains to his or her organization, whether it is a corporation or an institution)
- Students of human resources or business administration
- Workers (blue-collar or white-collar), staff, or management
- Professional association or labor organization staffers.

Using This Workbook

This workbook is designed to give the user maximum flexibility in choosing to read the background material in *Future Work*. The text may be read before or after the exercises.

Exercises are presented here for the themes and trends in the book, which are designated here in the same way as in the main text. Using these designations, the user can refer back to the text.

The exercise pages often start with illustrative data as a jumping-off point. The main text can be referred to for detailed data and for examples of implications for organizations. Many exercises include examples in the workspace, to illustrate the kinds of responses desired. The user may choose to endorse the sample answers or cross them out as wrong or of less significance to his or her organization.

This workbook is designed to be used by an individual or by a group, in a workshop format, or, in some cases, as a basis for group discussion. Many of the work pages end with questions that lend themselves to private thought or group discussion.

At many points in the workbook, we ask the user to provide or determine answers to questions about the organization he or she is considering or the region of the country in which it is located. Users may find that they do not have sufficient information to give more than rough answers. A guess or an estimate is sufficient for the purposes of this workbook. Another option, however, is to explore local and national public information or corporate or organizational data sources, to find out more. The section titled "Further Resources: Digging Deeper and Keeping Up-To-Date" at the end of *Future Work* provides some additional clues to external information sources. Many of the activities may lead the user to draw a diagram, lay out columns, or produce some other figure or chart, as an alternative to a discursive response.

Many exercises are loosely linked, forward and backward, to other exercises. For example, material relating to home life and work life may make reference to the exercises on cost-containment issues. However, it is not necessary to complete one exercise before moving on to another. The exercises may be worked in any order.

The sets of exercises for each theme or trend section should take between ten and fifteen minutes to complete. The time will vary according to the user's levels of knowledge and interest.

There is no one correct answer to any question raised in this workbook. The workbook is strongly future-oriented. In many cases, information is provided as a jumping-off point. *Future Work* provides additional information, including some implications and action opportunities for each trend.

The overarching aim of this workbook is to stimulate the user to think more systematically and broadly, and farther into the future, about human resources. With awareness of the wide range of possible outcomes, users should be stimulated to move on to more data gathering, analysis, and innovative adoption and experimentation in their own organizations. After doing the exercises in this book, users may find themselves to be enthusiastic advocates of innovation in the workplace.

THE AUTHORS

Joseph F. Coates is president of J. F. Coates, Inc., and adjunct professor at George Washington University, where he teaches graduate courses on technology and on the future. He received his B.S. degree (1951) from Brooklyn Polytechnic Institute in chemistry and his M.S. degree (1953) from Pennsylvania State University in organic chemistry. He holds an honorary degree from Claremont Graduate School.

Coates's principal current work is the study of the future. J. F. Coates, Inc., founded ten years ago, has produced more than seventy studies of the future, including several reports on the future of the work force. His other areas of interest are technology assessment, scientific and technological innovation, strategic planning, and issues management. In 1985, he and his associates received the Rose-Hulman Award from the International Association for Impact Assessment. Coates is coauthor of *What Futurists Believe* (1989, with J. Jarratt) and *Issues Management: How You Can Plan, Organize, and Manage for the Future* (1986, with others).

Coates was assistant to the director and head of exploratory research at the United States Congress Office of Technology Assessment from 1974 to 1979, manager of a research program at the National Science Foundation from 1970 to 1974, senior staff member of the Institute for Defense Analyses from 1962 to 1970, and industrial chemist at Atlantic Refining Company from 1953 to 1960. He holds nineteen patents.

Jennifer Jarratt is vice-president of J. F. Coates, Inc. She received her B.A. degree (1974) from Goddard College in fine arts and her M.S. degree (1989) from the University of Houston, Clear Lake, in studies of the future.

Jarratt's main research activities have been in the study of the future. She has participated in at least twenty projects, six on the future of the work force, since joining J. F. Coates, Inc., in 1983. Her other areas of interest include the environment, telecommunications and computers, social change, and issues management. Jarratt is coauthor of *What Futurists Believe* (1989, with J. F. Coates) and *Issues Management: How You Can Plan, Organize, and Manage for the Future* (1986, with others).

Jarratt was director of communications for the Planned Parenthood League of Connecticut from 1975 to 1982, feature writer on the Detroit Free Press from 1965 to 1971, and reporter and feature writer for the Sheffield Morning Telegraph (Sheffield, England) from 1962 to 1965.

John B. Mahaffie is an associate of J. F. Coates, Inc. He received his B.A. degree (1981) from the University of Pennsylvania in anthropology, an M.A. degree (1984) from the University of Arizona in anthropology, and another M.A. degree (1988) from George Washington University in international affairs.

Mahaffie has participated in ten studies of the future, two on the future of the work force, since joining J. F. Coates, Inc., in 1986. His other research activities include studies of informal sector economies, Third World economic development, and future applications of telecommunications. He also has been involved in American Indian affairs, Indian law, and federal Indian programs. In 1987, he was awarded a Presidential Management Internship.

Workbook to Accompany
Future Work

THEME 1

Increasing Diversity in the Work Force: Making Heterogeneity and Flexible Management Work

The American workplace is increasingly diverse in terms of aging, immigration, and the relative success of minorities. In the face of change and diversity, flexibility is demanded of management.

Some Data

Table 1. The Increasing Diversity of the U.S. Labor Force (Percentage of Total U.S. Labor Force by Race, Gender, and Ethnicity).

	1980	1995	Your Organization Today
White men	51.0	46.0	
White women	36.6	38.2	
Black men	5.2	5.6	
Black women	5.0	5.9	
Hispanic men	3.6	5.3	
Hispanic women	2.1	3.6	
Males	57.5	53.5	
Females	42.6	46.5	

Source: Data from U.S. Bureau of the Census. Statistical Abstract of the United States, 1989. Washington, D.C.: GPO, 1989, p. 376.

1. Assess the diversity of your organization. (It is not necessary to be very accurate.)

   a. Divide the pyramid in Figure 1 into hierarchical layers by drawing horizontal lines across it. If you wish, you may indicate the relative size of a layer with the thickness of the bands you create.

   b. Label the layers in a way appropriate to the organization (for example, senior management, middle management, supervisors, sales force, factory workers).

   c. Divide each layer into vertical segments, and shade them at each level according to relative proportions of the ethnic groups indicated. Use the shadings indicated in the legend to the right of the figure.

Figure 1. The Ethnic Makeup of Your Work Force.

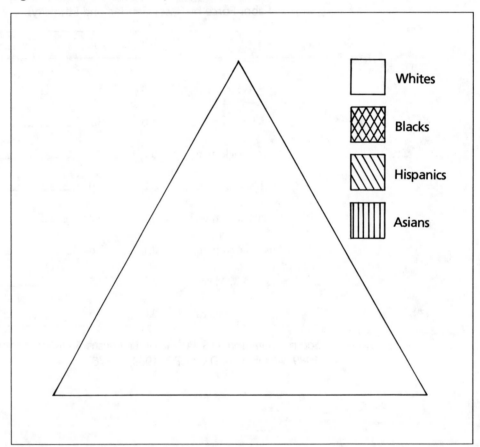

d. Now shade the pyramid in Figure 2 for the gender makeup of the work force. Use the shadings indicated in the legend to the right of the figure.

Figure 2. The Gender Makeup of Your Work Force.

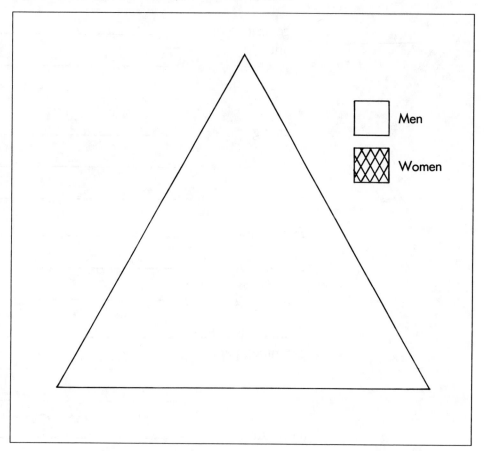

2. Describe how this pattern will change or should change over the next decade.

3. List two or three ways that diversity has affected and will affect each of the following areas.

	Has Affected	*Will Affect*
Organization of Work	_____	_____
	_____	_____
	_____	_____
Teaming	_____	_____
	_____	_____
	_____	_____
Supervision	_____	_____
	_____	_____
	_____	_____
Rewards (benefits, amenities, perks)	_____	_____
	_____	_____
	_____	_____
Recruitment	_____	_____
	_____	_____
	_____	_____
Retention	_____	_____
	_____	_____
	_____	_____

Discussion

Does the work force of the organization under consideration reflect the general makeup of the area's work force? If not, why may this be so? What new groups are rising in numbers in the work force? What are the implications for the organization and its work force? What may the organization need to do to accommodate new and rising numbers of ethnic- and minority-group workers, including women?

Continuing Aging of the Work Force
Creates Problems and Opportunities
for Human Resources

As the baby boom ages, the work force is aging. There are consequently
shortages of younger workers at the entry level. At the same time, baby-boom
values and attitudes are becoming predominant.

Some Data

Table 1-1.1. A Breakdown of the Civilian Labor Force by Age, 1987 (Percentage of
Total Labor Force for Each Age Group).

	Men	*Your Organization*	*Women*	*Your Organization*
16–19	3.4	_____	3.3	_____
20–24	6.5	_____	5.9	_____
25–34	16.4	_____	13.0	_____
35–44	13.0	_____	10.8	_____
45–54	8.5	_____	6.7	_____
55–64	5.8	_____	4.1	_____
65+	1.6	_____	1.0	_____

Source: Data from U.S. Bureau of the Census. *Statistical Abstract of the United States,
1989*. Washington, D.C.: GPO, 1989, p. 376.

1. The median age of the U.S. work force is about thirty-seven.

   a. How do you think your organization's work force compares? Circle your
       response.

                   younger   the same   older

   b. How has it changed in the past five years? Circle your response.

                   younger   no change   older

   c. How will it change in the next five years? Circle your response.

                   younger   no change   older

2. List the age groups that are most influential or important in your company, and identify what may change for them over the next ten years.

Groups	*Changes*
_____	_____
_____	_____
_____	_____
_____	_____
_____	_____

3. In each of the categories that follow, identify one or two human resources issues that may arise as your work force gets older.

Training/education/
skills

Obsolete skills, _____

_____

Equal employment
opportunities, women,
minorities

_____

_____

Management
development

_____

_____

Work-force
composition

_____

_____

Compensation,
benefits, amenities,
rewards

_____

_____

Labor relations

_____

_____

Productivity, quality,
performance

_____

Recruitment, retention   _____

_____

Return on investment   _____

_____

Facilities, siting   _____

_____

Human resources
planning, strategy   _____

_____

Restructuring   _____

_____

4. In light of an aging work force, respond to the following items for your organization.

    a. Has the baby bust (the shortage of people between eighteen and twenty-four) led to shortages of entry-level workers in your region? Will it in the next ten years?

    b. List some hiring practices that you can implement to ensure an adequate labor supply.

       Summer jobs/internships, _____

_____

_____

_____

_____

c. For your company, list ten consequences of the aging work force. Consider management, promotion, compensation, and other human resources issues.

_____

_____

_____

_____

_____

_____

_____

_____

d. Identify management practices that can help accommodate older workers.

_____

_____

_____

_____

_____

e. Are retirees a source of either part- or full-time workers? List the job categories in which they usually work or could work.

_____

_____

_____

_____

_____

_____

Discussion

Besides more aggressive recruiting, what can be done in the face of the labor shortage?

TREND 1-2	Older Americans Increase in Number and Grow in Influence

Older Americans are richer, more numerous, and more powerful today than in the past.

Some Data

- *The elderly are numerous.* Those sixty-five and over comprise 12.4 percent of the U.S. population, about 31 million people. The median age in the United States is thirty-three years.
- *The elderly are not poor.* Only 12.2 percent of the elderly lived below the poverty line by 1987. Their median household income was $14,330.
- *Many older Americans work.* About 12.5 percent—15 million of the civilian labor force—are fifty-five and older; 3 million of these are sixty-five and older (about 2.6 percent of the labor force).

Sources: Data from Carter Henderson, "Old Glory: America Comes of Age," *The Futurist*, 1988, *22* (2), 37; U.S. Department of Commerce, Bureau of the Census, *Statistical Abstract of the United States, 1989.* Washington, D.C.: GPO, 1989, p. 454; and U.S. Department of Commerce, Bureau of the Census, "Population Profile of the United States," *Current Population Reports*, ser. P-23, no. 159. Washington, D.C.: GPO, 1989; and personal communication with U.S. Bureau of the Census, July 1989.

Table 1-2.1. A Breakdown of the U.S. Population by Region, 1990 (Percentage of Total Regional Population for Each Age Group).

	Under 5	5–17	18–24	25–44
Northeast	6.7	16.8	10.1	32.2
Midwest	7.5	18.6	10.2	32.1
South	7.3	18.6	10.6	32.2
West	7.9	18.7	10.4	34.3

Source: Data from U.S. Bureau of the Census. *Statistical Abstract of the United States, 1989.* Washington, D.C.: GPO, 1989, p. 25.

1. List ways in which the aging of America may affect the work force, marketing, and benefits in your organization.

Work Force

More workers caring for elderly relatives,

_____

_____

_____

_____

Marketing

_____

_____

_____

_____

Benefits

_____

_____

_____

_____

2. How can your company serve an aging American market?

   Large-print instruction books,

   _____

   _____

   _____

   _____

   _____

3. Would older workers serve your organization better in its interaction with older customers?

Hispanics are a significant and growing ethnic group in the United States. They are a multifaceted market and segment of the work force. Some regions of the country are either largely Hispanic or have substantial Hispanic neighborhoods in their major cities. Mark your organization's location or locations in the United States on the map shown in Figure 1-3.1, and consider their proximity to the Hispanic population of the country.

Figure 1-3.1. Percentage of Hispanic Population.

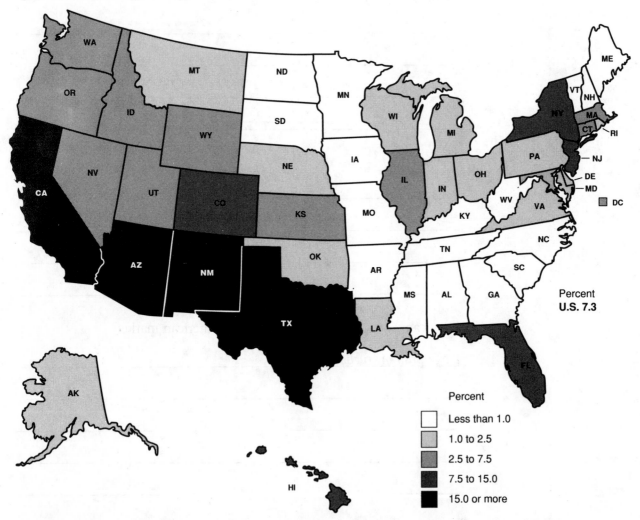

Percent
U.S. 7.3

Percent
- Less than 1.0
- 1.0 to 2.5
- 2.5 to 7.5
- 7.5 to 15.0
- 15.0 or more

Source: U.S. Bureau of the Census. "Population Estimates by Race and Hispanic Origin for States, Metropolitan Areas, and Selected Countries: 1980 to 1985. *Current Population Reports*, ser. p-25, no. 1040-RD-1. Washington, D.C.: GPO, 1989, p. 65.

1. Do you manufacture or market in any of the major Hispanic regions in the United States?

2. *Hispanic* is a misleading catchall term. Check which of the following Hispanic groups you hire and market to. Note the distinguishing characteristics we have identified for those groups.

	Work Force	*Market*	*Distinguishing Characteristics*
a. "New" Mexican	_____	_____	Recent immigrant or illegal status; economic refugees; proximity to native country; long-term ethnic roots in some U.S. cities
b. "Old" Mexican (Chicano)	_____	_____	Native to United States; likely bilingual; ethnic regions; wide range on the economic ladder
c. Central American	_____	_____	Recent immigrant or illegal status; political refugees; interest in native country, political progress

d. South   _____   _____   More likely to be
   American   educated, skilled

e. Cuban   _____   _____   Focus on Miami;
                                                     political refugees;
                                                     children divided
                                                     into well-
                                                     established
                                                     immigrant group
                                                     and recent
                                                     Marielitos; most
                                                     well educated,
                                                     older, and
                                                     prosperous

f. Puerto Rican   _____   _____   Concentrated in
                                                     Northeast and on
                                                     the island; all
                                                     citizens; can visit
                                                     home readily

g. Spanish   _____   _____   Likely to be
                                                     educated; legal,
                                                     permanent
                                                     immigrants

3. Compare your Hispanic and non-Hispanic work forces for their similarities
   and differences.

Similarities	*Differences*
_____	_____
_____	_____
_____	_____
_____	_____
_____	_____
_____	_____
_____	_____

4. List some human resources issues you have encountered, or see emerging in the next decade, involving the rise of Hispanics in your work force. Identify desirable (a) and undesirable (b) human resources responses for each.

Issues	*Human Resources Responses*
_____	a. _____
	b. _____
_____	a. _____
	b. _____
_____	a. _____
	b. _____
_____	a. _____
	b. _____
_____	a. _____
	b. _____

Discussion

Has your organization tapped into the Hispanic community, either as a labor force or as a market? What are some of the ways it could do so?

Do your marketing techniques recognize diversity within the Hispanic market?

Does your community support Hispanics culturally and linguistically?

Black America Experiences Multiple
Transitions

About 70 percent of black Americans are making it in society and in the
workplace. However, obstacles to black progress still remain.

Some Data

Table 1-4.1. A Comparison of Blacks and Whites.

	Blacks	Whites
Percent of total population (1987)	12.2	84.1
Percent of total labor force (1987)	10.8	86.2
Median age of population	27.2	33.0
High school completion rate (1987) (25- to 34-year-olds)	81.7	87.2
Labor force participation rate (1988)		
Men	71.0	76.9
Women	58.0	56.4
Median household income (1987)	$20,743	$33,526

Source: Data from U.S. Bureau of the Census. *Statistical Abstract of the United States,
1989.* Washington, D.C.: GPO, 1989, pp. 16, 133, 377, and 440; U.S. Bureau of Labor
Statistics. Personal communication, August 1989.

List the strengths and weaknesses behind the progress of blacks in your
organization's work force. Suggest an implied human resources action to
capitalize on each strength and to overcome each weakness.

Strengths   *Implied Human Resources Actions*

_____   _____

                        _____

_____   _____

                        _____

_____   _____

                        _____

_____   _____

                        _____

_____   _____

                                _____

Weaknesses   *Implied Human Resources Actions*

_____   _____

                                _____

_____   _____

                                _____

_____   _____

                                _____

_____   _____

                                _____

_____   _____

                                _____

Discussion

In many of the states, there are concentrations of very poor blacks in urban ghettos. These workers are often poorly educated and poorly acculturated to job skills, and they have histories of chronic unemployment. Is this a situation in your community? How is this affecting your business? Your work force? What could your company begin to do to change this situation?

TREND 1-5	Women Move Gradually into the Executive Suite

Women in management and professional ranks are succeeding as never before in the organization. However, many still encounter barriers to advancement when they reach middle or upper management. They bump up against what is known as a *glass ceiling*, an organizational obstacle to their progress, such as a lack of operational experience. Blacks, Hispanics, and Asians sometimes encounter such a ceiling as well.

Some Data

Table 1-5.1. Women as a Percentage of Total Employment by Occupation, 1987.

Ownership of small businesses (1986)	29.9
Managerial and professional specialties	44.3
Technical, sales, and administrative support	64.7
Service occupations	60.6
Precision production, craft, and repair	8.5
Operators, fabricators, and laborers	25.8
Farming, forestry, and fishing	15.8

Source: Data from the U.S. Bureau of the Census. *Statistical Abstract of the United States, 1989.* Washington, D.C.: GPO, 1989, p. 388; U.S. Small Business Administration. *The State of Small Business: A Report of the President.* Washington, D.C.: GPO, 1989, p. 27.

1. Estimate how women are distributed in your organization, and suggest a target percentage of women in each relevant job category.

Job Category	Estimated Percentage of Women	Targeted Percentage of Women
_____	_____	_____
_____	_____	_____
_____	_____	_____
_____	_____	_____
_____	_____	_____

2. Is there a glass ceiling in your organization? Do women rise to a certain level and then find that they can go no farther upward?

    a. Describe the situation.

    b. What could be done about it? List some human resources steps for addressing the problem.

_____

_____

_____

_____

_____

_____

3. Mark how high up the glass ceiling is in your organization. Place an *X* in the grid at the level that reflects the ceiling for women, as well as for blacks, Hispanics, Asians, and others.

	Women	Blacks	Hispanics	Asians	Others
Board of directors					
Chief executive officer					
Senior vice-presidents					
Vice-presidents					
Senior managers					
Middle managers					
Junior managers					
Foremen					
Supervisors					

4. How do you expect this situation to change in the next decade? Will the line move up? Disappear? Circle your response.

move up   move down   remain the same   disappear

5. List human resources actions or programs that could cause this situation to change.

A mentoring program for women managers, _____

_____

_____

_____

_____

Discussion

Is it easy for your organization to attract and keep top-quality women?

CEOs of one hundred *Fortune* 500 industrial and service companies were polled on the chances of women becoming CEO of their companies by the year 2000: poor, 40 percent; fair, 40 percent; good, 20 percent. (Saporito, B. "The Fortune 500 CEO Poll," *Fortune*, Sept. 28, 1987, p. 58.) How about your organization?

Are any jobs in your organization feminized (routinely staffed by women)? Why would this matter? Will it change over the next decade?

How equitably does your organization treat women? Has this situation affected your ability to recruit women?

High-Achieving Asians Are Outperforming North American Whites in the Classroom and the Workplace

The Asian-American population is rising fast, outpacing the growth of other ethnic groups. Political and social events in Asia are fueling the immigration of many more Asians to North America. Table 1-6.1. shows rates of high school completion for five Asian-American groups; the rate for whites is 87 percent.

Some Data

Table 1-6.1. **High School Completion Rates for Asian-Americans.**

Japanese (males)	96%
Koreans	94%
Indians	94%
Chinese	90%
Filipinos	89%

Source: Data from American Management Association. *Successful Marketing to U.S. Hispanics and Asians*. Washington, D.C.: A.M.A., 1987, p. 81.

1. Is your organization using or recruiting Asians as much as it should? Compare your organization to local industry norms.

2. List the strengths and weaknesses behind the progress of Asians in your organization's work force. Suggest an implied human resources action to capitalize on each strength and to overcome each weakness.

Strengths	*Implied Human Resources Actions*
_____	_____
_____	_____
_____	_____
_____	_____
_____	_____

Weaknesses	*Implied Human Resources Actions*
_____	_____
_____	_____
_____	_____
_____	_____
_____	_____

A Shrinking Labor Pool Creates Opportunities for Traditionally Underemployed Workers

The shrinking entry-level labor pool in the United States means that certain traditionally underemployed categories of workers are increasingly important to the organization.

Some Data

Table 1-7.1. U.S. Totals for Some Categories of Traditionally Underemployed Workers (in Thousands).

The work disabled (1988)	13,420
Involuntary part-time workers (1986)	5,300
Displaced workers (1986)	5,130
High school dropouts (1987)	4,252
Probationers (1986)	2,094
Elderly in labor force (1987)	1,200
Unemployed, discouraged (1986)	1,100
Recent parolees (1986)	327

Source: Data from U.S. Bureau of the Census. *Statistical Abstract of the United States, 1989.* Washington, D.C.: GPO, 1989, pp. 146, 184, 360, and 376; U.S. Bureau of Labor Statistics. *Monthly Labor Review,* 1987, *110* (6); U.S. Bureau of Labor Statistics. *Monthly Labor Review,* 1987, *110* (9); *USA Today,* Jan. 29, 1988.

1. Consider the following scenario: Fred is a genius at his job. He can come up with brilliant, innovative ideas for developing new products. He is obnoxious, cannot work on a team, shows up late or sometimes not at all, says irrelevant things in the middle of meetings, and will not follow normal procedures for time sheets, in-house communications, or the office's computer system.

    a. In your organization, Fred would be (check one or more):

    _____ Fired   _____ Isolated

    _____ Demoted   _____ Tolerated

    _____ Promoted   _____ Celebrated

    _____ Closely managed and watched

    _____ Other: _____

b. What changes could be made to make a person like Fred more employable and useful to your organization?

A program of worker autonomy, _____

_____

_____

_____

_____

_____

2. On the following table, showing traditionally underutilized kinds of workers, mark those who are already employed by your organization, those who would be readily hired, and those for whom there are significant barriers to hiring.

	Already Employed	*Readily Hired*	*Significant Barriers*	*Where would they fit?*
Disabled or physically handicapped	_____	_____	_____	_____
Emotionally unstable	_____	_____	_____	_____
Illiterate	_____	_____	_____	_____
Drug and alcohol abusers	_____	_____	_____	_____
Ex-offenders	_____	_____	_____	_____
Homebound	_____	_____	_____	_____
Young urban poor	_____	_____	_____	_____
Functionally illiterate	_____	_____	_____	_____
Attitude problems, antisocial	_____	_____	_____	_____
Displaced, with no marketable skills	_____	_____	_____	_____

Discouraged   _____   _____   _____   _____
workers,
with few or
obsolete
skills

Transients,   _____   _____   _____   _____
or "rolling
stones"

Part-time,   _____   _____   _____   _____
wanting to
be full-time

Talented   _____   _____   _____   _____
misfits

Older   _____   _____   _____   _____
workers
unable or
unwilling to
learn new
skills

Retirees   _____   _____   _____   _____

Others ____   _____   _____   _____   _____

                  _____   _____   _____   _____

3. Could your organization use traditionally underutilized workers to fill positions left vacant by the labor shortage? If you could use them, what approaches might be used? Circle or fill in your responses.

More training

Special treatment

Close supervision

Careful placement

A buddy system

_____

_____

TREND 1-8 | The Scientific and Engineering Work Force Is Growing and Becoming More Diverse in National Origin, Gender, and Race

There are sometimes acute shortages of scientists, engineers, and technical workers in the United States. These workers have the lowest unemployment rates.

1. In the pie chart on the left of Figure 1-8.1, fill in the present distribution of scientists, engineers, and technicians in your work force. In the pie chart on the right, indicate what you think that distribution will be in the year 2000. What recruitment opportunities and challenges does the situation present?

Figure 1-8.1. Distribution of Scientists, Engineers, and Technicians.

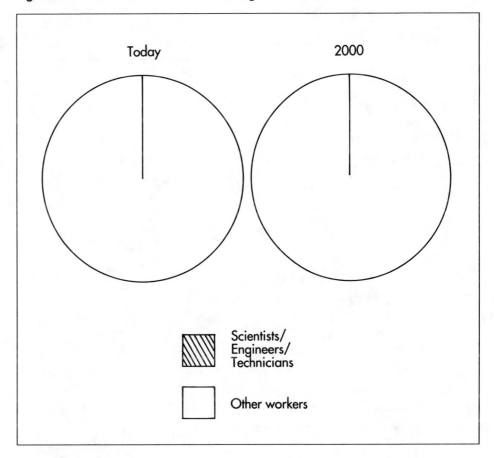

2. Identify practices in planning, management, and recruitment that your organization could use in the next decade to offset a shortage of these workers.

_____ In-house skill development

_____ Reaching into the schools to promote skills

_____ Recruiting foreign scientists and engineers

_____ Others _____

_____

_____

_____

_____

_____

THEME 2

Reintegrating Home Life and Work Life: Reversing a One Hundred-Year Trend

Reversing a one hundred-year trend, in which home and work life were kept sharply separated, workers today are reintegrating their home and work lives.

1. Rate the items in the following list according to their importance to your work force, using the designations *high*, *medium*, and *low*. You may choose to leave some out, as well as adding some new items to the list.

_____ a.   Health and fitness

_____ b.   Child care

_____ c.   Elder care

_____ d.   Education

_____ e.   Training

_____ f.   Family education/ training

_____ g.   Self-fulfillment

_____ h.   Drug and alcohol programs

_____ i.   Family finances

_____ j.   Sports and recreation events

_____ k.   Childbearing/fertility

_____ l.   Career planning

_____ m.   Relocation/housing assistance

_____ n.   Attendance

_____ o.   Avocations

_____ p.   Voluntary associations (for example, Boy Scouts)

_____ q.   _____

_____ r.   _____

_____ s.   _____

_____ t.   _____

_____ u.   _____

2. What is your company doing, or what could it do, to more effectively address these important concerns of the work force? How is the failure to meet these needs affecting the quality, performance, and morale of the work force?

3. In your own personal situation, what are the two or three most important family-related matters that influence or affect your work?

4. Personal concerns can affect the workplace to varying degrees. In creating the following Venn diagram, you can illustrate how they do so in your organization.

   a. Draw a diagram of two circles, to show how much overlap there is between work life and home life for the organization's workers. (The diagram may have no overlap, a complete overlap, or some degree of overlap in between.) Look at the following examples.

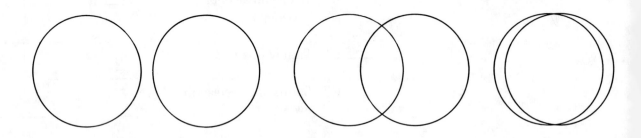

b. Label the circles "Home life" and "Work life."

c. Place letters from the list in exercise 1 to represent issues that you have identified as important in either the "Home life" or the "Work life" circle, or in the overlapping area. Place letters in the overlapping area for those issues that you believe are critical to both home and work life.

d. For any items in the overlapping area, what organizational functions and departments are responsible or should be responsible? Here, list the items and the parts or programs of the organization that should be involved.

Items	*Department/Program*

Discussion

Considering the diversity of people in your company or organization, how could new flexibility be achieved to meet the needs of the staff?

TREND 2-1	**Bringing Home to Work: Corporations Adopt New Programs to Support Employees' Family Responsibilities**	

Dual-earner families and working women with young children are pressuring organizations to support employees' family responsibilities (such as child and elder care).

1. Compare estimates for your organization to the national rates for the following items.

	Your Organization	National Rate	
Workers with a working spouse	_____%	67%	
Workers who care for an elderly relative	_____%	30%	(averaging 10 hours per week)
Workers who need day care for children.	_____%	13%	(7.1 million of the 53.7 million working women have children under 6)

Sources: Data from Morrison, P.A. "Families and the Workplace: Changing Demographic Realities." *Outlook*, San Francisco: Pacific Telesis Center, Feb. 1988.; U.S. Bureau of the Census. *Statistical Abstract of the United States, 1989*. Washington, D.C.: GPO, 1989, p. 386.; The Hay Group, "Forging a New Working Alliance: How to Meet the Broadened Human Resource Needs of the 1990s," Seminar, Chicago, Apr. 20, 1988.

2. Describe policies and programs that your organization has used to respond to the need for child care and elder care.

_____

_____

_____

_____

_____

_____

3. How could they be improved?

4. List how your ability to recruit and retain workers has and could have been affected by your organization's policies toward families.

How it has been affected

_____

_____

_____

_____

How it could have been affected

_____

_____

_____

_____

Work and Education Influence Women's Childbearing Choices and Shape National Fertility Patterns

Women are investing more in work and education. Childbearing can threaten their investment by removing them from the work force. At the same time, corporations can lose by losing part of their labor pool and their own investment in women's careers.

Some Data

Table 2-2.1. Births in the Past Year per 1,000 Women by Education and Occupation, 1987.

Category	Total Births per 1,000 Women
Not a high school graduate	92.7
High school, 4 years	71.6
College, 4 years	66.7
College, 5 or more years	58.4
In labor force	49.6
Not in labor force	128.0
Managerial-professional	48.1
Technical, sales, and administrative support	47.6
Service workers	46.2
Precision production, craft, and repair	26.7
Operators, fabricators, and laborers	47.7
Farming, forestry, and fishing	56.6

Source: Data from U.S. Bureau of the Census. Statistical Abstract of the United States, 1989. Washington, D.C.: GPO, 1989, p. 67.

1. Figure 2-2.1 shows forces influencing metropolitan areas. This kind of figure is called a *consequence diagram* or *signed digraph*. The arrows indicate the influence of forces on each other. The effects of the forces on each other are also labelled *positive* or *negative*. In Figure 2-2.2, try your hand at creating a similar diagram, showing the factors influencing working women's choice to have or not have a child. You may also choose to label the forces *positive* or *negative* as in Figure 2-2.1.

Figure 2-2.1. A Typical Signed Digraph.

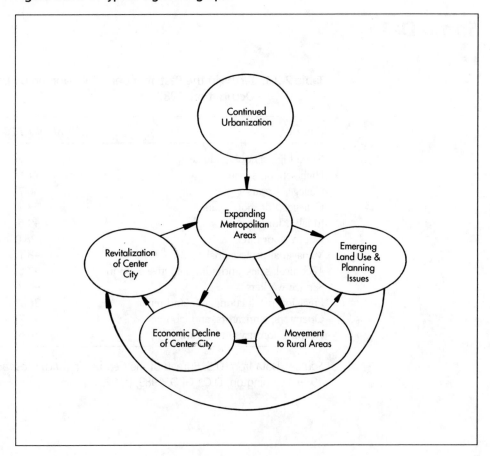

Figure 2-2.2. Factors Influencing Childbearing Choices.

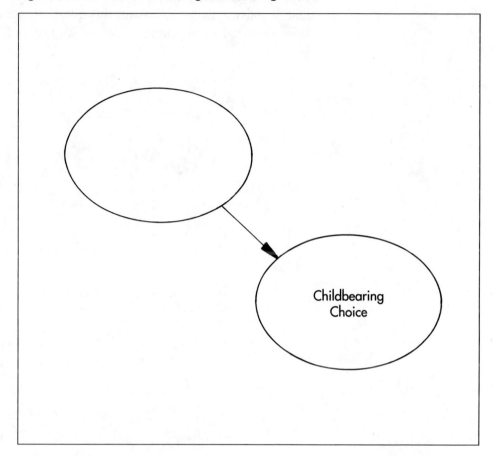

2. For the most important of the influence factors you included in Figure 2-2.2, indicate what your organization is doing or could do to influence a woman worker's childbearing decisions, particularly how the company could neutralize or prevent any negative effects on the woman's career path.

_____

_____

_____

_____

_____

_____

_____

3.Consider a woman you know whose career path has been either positively or negatively affected by childbearing, and write a brief account of that. If you are unable to answer this question, does that indicate that you have neglected an important aspect of your work force or your colleagues' lives?

TREND 2-3	Work Moves to Unconventional Sites and Arrangements

For many workers, it is now possible and desirable to work at new locations and under new and sometimes unconventional work arrangements. One such arrangement is work at home.

Some Data

Table 2-3.1. Contingent Workers in the United States, 1987 (in Millions).

Temporary workers	0.9
Part-time workers	19.5
Self-employed workers	9.6
Business-services workers	5.1
Total civilian labor force	119.9

Source: Data from Belous, R. "How Human Resource Systems Adjust to the Shift Toward Contingent Workers." U.S. Bureau of Labor Statistics, *Monthly Labor Review*, March 1989, p. 9.

1. List all the jobs or kinds of work in your organization that are or could be done at home.

_____

_____

_____

_____

_____

_____

2. Make two lists of other kinds of unconventional work or work arrangements, either at your own company or at other organizations (such as working in a customer's facility, working on the road, or working on a contract on a temporary basis). Then, consider the appeal and the benefits of each of those forms of work, and the negatives associated with them.

At My Company	*At Other Organizations*
_____	_____
_____	_____
_____	_____
_____	_____
_____	_____
_____	_____

3. Identify how these or other off-site arrangements affect management, productivity, and the exchange of information and ideas.

Management

Lack of direct supervision, _____

_____

_____

_____

Productivity

Information

---

4. Does your organization have or allow telecommuting? *Telecommuting* is the current term for performing electronic jobs (such as word processing) at home or outside the conventional office, with the linkage backed by a telephone line. People in telecommuting may work anywhere from one day to forty hours per week outside the traditional workplace.

5. Assume that telecommuting is well established in your organization. List some ways telecommuting affects your organization in terms of costs, savings, and ability to recruit workers.

---

6. Would flexibility in work arrangements be used to improve labor turnover and morale, and to reduce absenteeism?

7. List positions in your organization that could be filled by telecommuters.

_____

_____

_____

_____

_____

8. List positions that could be filled by workers participating in other work arrangements (job sharing, and so on).

Position	Arrangement
_____	_____
_____	_____
_____	_____
_____	_____

TREND 2-4	New Focus on the Worker as an Asset Makes Attitudes and Values More Central to Human Resources Planning

American workers are increasingly considered resources of the organization, rather than mere costs of doing business. As such, their values and attitudes are important to human resources planners.

1. Describe attitudes and values of the ideal worker in your organization over the next ten years.

   Strong customer-service orientation, _____

   _____

   _____

   _____

   _____

   _____

2. Name five values that benefit the work force and five that could be problems or obstacles.

   Positive Values

   _____

   _____

   _____

   _____

   _____

   Negative Values

   _____

   _____

   _____

   _____

Discussion

What could be done to reinforce and promote positive values? How have your own values, and the values of the people you are most familiar with, changed over the past decade, particularly in relation to work and the role of work in your life?

| # Mobility Continues to Be a Strength of the North American Work Force

American workers are highly mobile. This makes the work force highly flexible (assuming that mobility favors an organization). Workers' mobility can take two relevant directions: away from your area or into it. Hiring qualified workers may depend on the latter form of mobility.

1. List five qualities or amenities of your company's location that attract workers to the area.

Quality or Amenity	Worker Categories				
	Young	Older	Ethnics	Women	Specialists/ Experts
_____	_____	_____	_____	_____	_____
_____	_____	_____	_____	_____	_____
_____	_____	_____	_____	_____	_____
_____	_____	_____	_____	_____	_____
_____	_____	_____	_____	_____	_____

2. List five qualities that may make potential employees stay away.

_____	_____	_____	_____	_____	_____
_____	_____	_____	_____	_____	_____
_____	_____	_____	_____	_____	_____
_____	_____	_____	_____	_____	_____
_____	_____	_____	_____	_____	_____

3. How does or would your community stack up in the *Places Rated Almanac*?

4. List and discuss the three most important actions, from a human resources point of view, that your company could take to put it in a solid, effective, competitive position in the global economy.

Discussion

How can the organization improve the appeal of its immediate region and surroundings? Is it important for the organization to be active in community development? Whom must it work with? What are the key points of leverage? Need it cost money?

THEME 3

Globalization: Facing the Realities of Competing in a World Economy

The U.S. economy is increasingly integrated into the world economy. Globalization can be both an opportunity and a threat to the American corporation. Its effects encompass marketing, manufacturing, selling overseas, selling domestically, and other facets of the organization.

1. For your organization or industry, identify some opportunities you see emerging over the next decade in the global marketplace.

Opportunities	Human Resources Implications
_____	_____
_____	_____
_____	_____
_____	_____
_____	_____

2. Certain aspects of globalization may pose a threat to some industries in the United States. Describe some threats that you see affecting your industry and your company.

Threats	Human Resources Implications
_____	_____
_____	_____
_____	_____
_____	_____
_____	_____

Discussion

How could joint ventures with foreign companies benefit your organization in terms of goodwill, experience, access to new markets, and so on?

TREND 3-1	Mergers and Acquisitions Continue— with More Foreign Actors Involved

Mergers and acquisitions are putting corporate America into a constant state of flux, affecting companies and their competitors. Uncertainty affects everyone.

1. In the environment of mergers and acquisitions, uncertainties proliferate. What does this mean to the work force? What is the role of human resources in this environment?

2. Assume that your organization is involved in an acquisition. Define a ten-point human resources program for each of the following two situations.

You are acquired

_____

_____

_____

_____

_____

_____

_____

_____

_____

_____

You acquire another company

_____

_____

_____

_____

_____

_____

_____

_____

_____

_____

Discussion

If your company were acquired, whom would you like to be acquired by? Specify the pros and cons. Whom would you least like to be acquired by? Specify the pros and cons. In responding to this question, take a five- or ten-year perspective. You may find it revealing also to enumerate the winners and losers in such situations.

TREND 3-2	Work-Force and Market Demographics in Europe and Asia Present New Opportunities

The work forces of Europe and Asia are growing in education, sophistication, and spending power. At the same time, political and regulatory changes abroad are opening up new markets to American companies. As the globe becomes increasingly integrated, profound political and social changes are happening in many regions. These increasingly affect U.S. corporations, at home as well as abroad.

Figure 3-2.1. Map of the World.

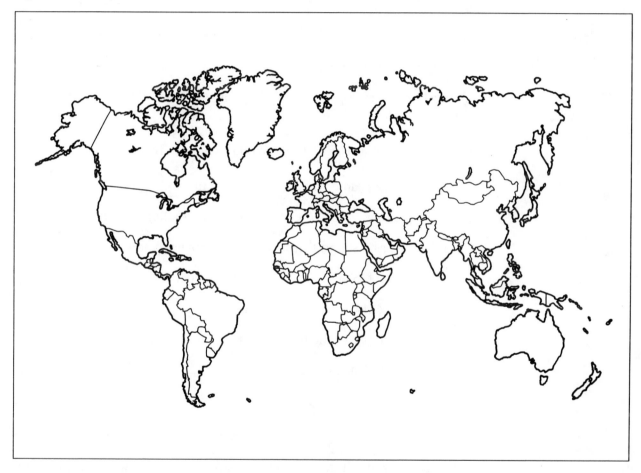

1. Over the next fifteen years, where outside the United States will your organization do the most new business?

    a. Mark the locations on the world map in Figure 3-2.1.

b. Identify implications of the growing importance of each world region you
    have identified.

Area   *Implications*

_____   _____

_____   _____

_____   _____

_____   _____

_____   _____

_____   _____

_____   _____

2. Check the developments in the following list that will affect your
    organization.

The Changing World Economic Scene

_____ European economic integration in 1992

_____ Hong Kong's reversion to the People's Republic of China

_____ Glasnost and Perestroika in the Soviet Union

_____ The U.S.–Canada Free Trade Agreement

_____ The rise of Asian economies

_____ The rise of the newly industrialized countries (NICs)

_____ Other factors _____

                _____

                _____

3. List some of the human resources issues associated with the preceding
    factors.

_____

_____

_____

_____

_____

4. Name some country you are likely to move into for manufacturing, marketing, joint ventures, or other business activities. List the fifteen most important human resources considerations that would enter into planning for that intervention.

   Country: _____

   _____

   _____

   _____

   _____

   _____

   _____

   _____

   _____

   _____

   _____

   _____

   _____

   _____

   _____

5. Insofar as there are any gaps in your response to question 4, what are plausible specific ways to begin to close those gaps?

Discussion

In what year is it likely or possible that a non-American will head your organization?

Sweeping Changes Are Altering Market Basics

The world of marketing is increasingly complex, given changes in society, demography, and the world. The goal of marketing should continue to be to meet the customer on his or her own terms, in the correct language and style, and at the right time. Profile your marketing and market in the following four exercises.

1. *Who is doing the selling?*

   Women _____ %

   Men _____ %

   Young (20–45) _____ %

   Old (46+) _____ %

   Hispanics _____ %

   Asians _____ %

   Blacks _____ %

   Whites _____ %

2. *Who are the customers?*

   Women _____ %

   Men _____ %

   Young (20–45) _____ %

   Old (46+) _____ %

   Hispanics _____ %

   Asians _____ %

   Blacks _____ %

   Whites _____ %

3. *When is the selling done?*
   (Check all that apply.)

   Daytime _____

   Nighttime _____

   By phone _____

   By mail _____

   On the air _____

4. *When customers receptive?*
   (Check all that apply.)

   Daytime _____

   Nighttime _____

   At work _____

   At home _____

   On the road _____

5. Should salespeople sell to "their own kind"? Why or why not?

6. Assess the matchup in your organization between product and market for the following factors.

   a. Product style and packaging (or how service is performed)

   b. Language(s) used in advertising, packaging

   c. Regional interests, differences

   d. Household types targeted

7. List five specific human resources actions or developments that can contribute to a better fit between sales force and marketplace.

_____

_____

_____

_____

_____

_____

Discussion

One dimension of change in marketing is the profound demographic change faced by most organizations. How does your sales staff compare demographically with your market? Should the sales force closely mirror the market demographically?

Worldwide Technical and Scientific Competence Will Sharpen Competition

The rest of the world is catching up with the United States in scientific and technological competence. Competition is heating up.

1. Today, and ten years from now, what technical or scientific job skills are and will be important to your organization? List those that are or will be most difficult to find.

Today	2000
_____	_____
_____	_____
_____	_____
_____	_____
_____	_____
_____	_____
_____	_____

2. Describe human resources steps and strategies for preparing your work force for sharper competition in the world marketplace.

3. Have you had experience with international recruitment?

4. How would you begin a program for international recruitment? List some steps.

_____

_____

_____

_____

_____

_____

_____

_____

5. What are the pros and cons of international recruitment? (Three examples of each are given.)

Pros	*Cons*
Skills are found	Paperwork
May be U.S.-trained	Long lead time
Strong work ethic	Language barriers

_____ _____

_____ _____

_____ _____

_____ _____

_____ _____

Discussion

Define a complete human resources strategy to fill the critical need for science and technology skills in your organization.

THEME 4

Expanding Human Resources Planning: Restructuring Roles and Practices to Improve Business-Unit Planning

Many of the pressures on organizations, today and in the future, are and will be focused on the work force. Human resources has an expanding role in steering the organization and its workers through the waves of change affecting them.

1. Identify human resources roles in the following grid. Place a mark in the grid for each of the organizational goals (listed across the top) that corresponds to a human resources function (listed on the left).

	Innovation in rewards	Changes in compensation	New kinds of leadership	Worker empowerment	Intrapreneur-ship	Downsizing
Exploring workers' attitudes and desires						
Identifying candidates						
Overseeing equity and fairness						
Monitoring effectiveness of programs						
Identifying workers' needs						
Work-force demographics						
Long-term benefits planning						
Career development and planning						
Training and education						
Educating workers on programs and practices						

2. Is your human resources staff prepared to perform these roles? List some areas where human resources in your organization needs to advance its own training and skill bases.

_____

_____

_____

_____

_____

_____

_____

3. What important business-planning information did you have in the past six to twelve months that you felt was important to deliver to top managers, senior managers, business-unit planners, or others? How exactly did you go about doing it? How effective were you? What kinds of improvement could have been made in the steps you took? What will you do differently next time?

TREND 4-1 | Human Resources Forges New Roles for Itself in a Changing Business World

Human resources is an evolving profession, striving to keep pace with change in the workplace. Human resources today is traditionally involved with the following areas:

Compensation and benefits
Human resources planning,
  strategy
Return on investment
Equal employment opportunities,
  women, minorities
Labor relations
Productivity, quality, performance

Recruitment, retention
Restructuring
Training, education, management
  development
Work-force composition
Skills

1. Among the new roles expanding the human resources profession are the following. Which of these roles have emerged in your human resources department? Check the appropriate items.

  _____ Corporate strategic planner

  _____ College faculty member/administrator

  _____ Temporary-agency administrator

  _____ Psychologist/stress-management adviser

  _____ Innovation promoter

  _____ Career- and life-planning adviser

  _____ Cultural anthropologist

  _____ Testing-service operator

  _____ Corporate demographer

  _____ Employee assistance program coordinator and adviser

  _____ Lawyer/regulation interpreter

  _____ Lobbyist

  _____ Counselor to top management

  _____ Engineer/technologist

2. Why have these roles emerged in your organization? Would you like to fill these jobs?

3. Write down the roles that you think could be most important. How will persons filling such roles serve the organization?

Roles	*How They Will Serve*
_____	_____
_____	_____
_____	_____
_____	_____
_____	_____

4. List any other nontraditional human resources roles that you believe have emerged or will emerge.

5. Write an advertisement for a human resources manager in your organization for the year 2000.

Discussion

Do the new roles for human resources make sense? Which of them should be performed by other departments, and which by outside contractors and consultants?

| # The Corporation Is Increasingly Committed to Improving Performance Through Innovation in Rewards

Competing for a shrinking labor pool, and getting the best out of workers at all levels, demands innovation in rewards.

1. Check any constraints on innovation in rewards in your organization.

   _____ Worries about fairness

   _____ Unions—agreements and pressures

   _____ Lack of creativity in management

   _____ Workers' attitudes

   _____ Management's attitudes

   _____ Corporate culture (never have done it before; not a fun-and-games workplace)

2. Identify some steps to improve innovation in rewards.

   _____

   _____

   _____

   _____

   _____

   _____

3. Name the most satisfying or innovative reward(s) you have received or heard of in your organization or another.

4. What would be the best possible way to be rewarded (the most attractive nonmonetary reward)?

Discussion

How would you go about finding out what kinds of rewards the workers in your organization would particularly like to have? Keep in mind that they have been accustomed mostly to either monetary equivalents or symbolic rewards. How would you open the door to thinking about broader opportunities?

TREND 4-3	Organizational and Work-Force Restructuring Leads to Changes in Compensation

The changing goals of the organization are forcing employers to reconsider and reshape their compensation patterns.

1. Which of the following nontraditional forms of compensation would your firm consider?

   _____ Cash bonuses

   _____ ESOPs

   _____ Profit sharing

   _____ Group incentives

   _____ Pay for knowledge

   _____ Pay for performance

   _____ Earned time off

   _____ Early retirement

   _____ Others _____

   _____

2. How does or could your organization discover what rewards its workers would like? List the steps involved.

   _____

   _____

   _____

   _____

   _____

3. List two or three alternative and new possibilities for forms of compensation that could benefit workers and the organization where you work.

   _____

   _____

   _____

Discussion

Discuss money as a reward, from the point of view of both its monetary and its symbolic value. How can one make more effective use of each of these key values associated with money?

| TREND 4-4 | The Search Intensifies for Venturesome Corporate Leadership |

Appropriate leadership is essential to the organization facing local, national, and global challenges.

1. Assess the current leadership of your organization. Which of the following characterizations describes the CEO?

_____ *Traditional*: Tends to rely on the hierarchy and structure of the organization to enforce direction. May be almost invisible to outsiders.

_____ *Transactional*: Participatory, listening style. Has long-range view, fronts to the outside world. Adept in working with people, groups. Inspiring; a model.

_____ *Transformational*: Visionary. May be evangelical about vision for the organization. Can be impatient, not always easy to get along with. Lives by results. An inspiration and a model, usually after his or her departure.

2. Explain why you made your choice of characterization for your CEO. What do you gain from having such a leader?

3. In your own experience, what person has shown the greatest leadership? List that person's strengths and weaknesses.

Strengths	*Weaknesses*
_____	_____
_____	_____
_____	_____
_____	_____

4. If you were able to deliver a confidential message to your CEO about his or her strengths and weaknesses, what would that message be?

5. List the units of your organization that you think are in need of new leadership. Why do they need it?

Unit	Why new leadership is needed
_____	_____
_____	_____
_____	_____
_____	_____
_____	_____

6. Consider the characterizations of leadership style in exercise 1 for the head of human resources in your organization. What style of leadership will be needed over the next decade? Why?

7. What kinds of leadership will your organization need over the next ten years?

CEO	Human Resources	
_____	_____	Traditional
_____	_____	Transactional
_____	_____	Transformational

8. Why will these kinds of leadership be needed?

CEO

_____

_____

_____

_____

Human Resources

_____

_____

_____

_____

| TREND 4-5 | Competition Promotes Intrapreneurship and Worker Empowerment |

In efforts to step up their competitiveness, U.S. corporations are giving workers more discretion, authority, autonomy, and information. Some, with intrapreneurship programs, are setting up programs to allow the energies of the entrepreneur to flourish inside the organization.

1. Is there room for intrapreneurship in your organization? List the divisions or tasks where this kind of arrangement makes sense.

_____

_____

_____

_____

_____

_____

_____

2. Identify some obstacles to intrapreneuring and worker empowerment in your organization.

_____

_____

_____

_____

_____

_____

_____

3. List five pros and five cons of worker empowerment.

   Pros

   _____

   _____

   _____

   _____

   _____

   Cons

   _____

   _____

   _____

   _____

   _____

4. If you were to start a program of intrapreneurship in your organization, exactly where would you begin, and how?

TREND 4-6 | Downsizing Reshuffles the Work-Force Deck

Perhaps because of a long period of payroll bloat, many U.S. corporations underwent downsizing in the past ten years. The impacts on workers and management practices give human resources new challenges: To clean up in the aftermath and work with newly streamlined organizations.

1. Consider the outcome, for your organization, of a 25 percent cut in the work force.

   a. Identify where the cuts could be made.

      _____

      _____

      _____

      _____

      _____

      _____

   b. List some steps that human resources should take to handle outplacement, phaseout of jobs (and people), and public relations in the aftermath of a major cutback.

      Outplacement

      _____

      _____

      _____

      _____

      _____

      Phaseout of Jobs

      _____

      _____

      _____

      _____

      _____

Public Relations

_____

_____

_____

_____

_____

c. The laid-off workers would find jobs in which of the following categories? (Choose one or more.)

_____   With our competitors

_____   In other cities

_____   In new fields

_____   Only after protracted search

2. List some measures that your organization could take to avoid further
depressing workers' morale during downsizing.

_____

_____

_____

_____

_____

_____

_____

3. How would you assess the consequences of downsizing for workplace morale and performance before, during, and after an episode of downsizing? In other words, how would you discover effects that you should be planning to enhance or mitigate?

THEME 5

The Changing Nature of Work: Training and Reeducating for a Knowledge-Based Work Force

Work is increasingly knowledge-based and rooted in information technologies. Technological change is ongoing and rapid. Globalization brings many workers into contact with their counterparts around the world. Workers must keep up (and must be kept up) in their knowledge and skills, to maintain their productivity on the job.

1. List some areas where your organization has experienced skill shortages.

_____

_____

_____

_____

_____

_____

_____

2. In which areas do you believe your organization will experience worker shortages in the future?

_____

_____

_____

_____

_____

_____

_____

_____

TREND 5-1 | New Critical Skills Are Emerging

The information-based future workplace will demand new skills. The work force's skill base has to keep pace with rapid economic and technological change.

1. Identify the following items for your organization.

   a. New, or newly important, critical skills

   Positive Skills or Attributes

   _____

   _____

   _____

   Technical Skills

   _____

   _____

   _____

   Specialty Skills

   _____

   _____

   _____

   Executive or Managerial Skills

   _____

   _____

   _____

b. Skills less likely to be wanted

Declining Skills

_____

_____

_____

Oversupplied Skills

_____

_____

_____

c. Skills that may become more necessary

_____

_____

_____

2. List steps that your organization could take to meet emerging skill needs.

In-House Skills

_____

_____

_____

Recruitment Skills

_____

_____

_____

Skills in the Community

_____

_____

_____

3. Consider the last five new employees of whom you have some personal knowledge. How do these new employees stack up against these emerging skills? Calling the employees *A, B, C, D,* and *E,* list the strengths and weaknesses that each brought to the job, in terms of knowledge, skills, training, capabilities, and other factors.

	Strengths	*Weaknesses*
A:	_____	_____
	_____	_____
	_____	_____
	_____	_____
B:	_____	_____
	_____	_____
	_____	_____
	_____	_____
C:	_____	_____
	_____	_____
	_____	_____
	_____	_____
D:	_____	_____
	_____	_____
	_____	_____
	_____	_____
E:	_____	_____
	_____	_____
	_____	_____
	_____	_____

| Training and Education Budgets Stay High as Corporations Stretch for New Results

Steady, thorough, career-long training is essential in keeping the worker up-to-date in a changing work world.

Some Data

Table 5-2.1. Hours of Training, by Job Category[a]

Job Category	Average Number of Hours per Year	Your Company
Middle managers	44	_____
Professionals	42	_____
Executives	41	_____
Salespeople	40	_____
First-line supervisors	40	_____
Senior managers	39	_____
Production workers	35	_____
Customer-service people	33	_____
Administrative personnel	22	_____
Office/clerical workers	18	_____

[a]Companies, with fifty or more employees, that provide training

Source: Data from *The Wall Street Journal*, July 17, 1987.

1. Compare the training record in your organization with the data shown in Table 5-2.1. For each category of worker, in the spaces provided, estimate whether your training is *more*, *less*, or the *same*. Is this enough training?

2. Identify the job categories in your organization that have critical training needs. What kinds of training are needed?

Positions	*Training Needs*
_____	_____
_____	_____
_____	_____
_____	_____

3. What training do *you* need?

4. How could training and education be built into work in your organization? Check off or name the programs that meet the skill, education, or training needs of your work force.

Needs	*Programs Regularly Used*	*Average Number of Hours per Year*
Literacy	_____	_____
Math literacy (numeracy)	_____	_____
Basic office skills	_____	_____
English	_____	_____
Foreign languages	_____	_____
Computer literacy	_____	_____
Self-help/personal growth	_____	_____

Cultural/gender sensitivity _____ _____

Team building _____ _____

Leadership _____ _____

Risk taking _____ _____

Executive development _____ _____

Other _____ _____ _____

5. In what areas could training improve productivity?

_____

_____

_____

_____

_____

_____

6. Name some number of specific job categories. In an ideal situation, how much training (in days per year) do your think workers in each category should be receiving each year? In addition to training, what about education? What is the difference?

TREND 5-3	The Corporation Reaches Deeper into the Educational System to Influence the Quality of Its Supply of Workers

Employers are finding a growing gap between their entry-level skill needs and the basic skill levels of their applicants.

Some Data

- Over one million students drop out of U.S. schools each year.
- An estimated 42 percent of those who finish high school are only marginally literate.
- By one estimate, supplying remedial training and job skills may be costing corporations $21 billion per year.

Source: Data from O'Rourke, J. "Education for the Future." Draft of a policy paper prepared for the Council of State Governments, 1987; *John Naisbitt's Trend Letter*, July 21, 1988, p. 8.

1. Does your local educational system deliver to your organization the levels of skills and education that you need in your employees? Assign letter grades (*A, B, C, D, F*) to each category of local schools.

   Elementary schools   _____

   Secondary schools   _____

   Trade schools   _____

   Community colleges   _____

   Universities   _____

2. Are you forced to recruit from out of town?

3. Do you have to "grow your own" – develop and educate workers through in-house training programs?

4. List practices or programs that your organization already uses to influence the educational system.

_____

_____

_____

_____

_____

_____

_____

_____

5. List other steps that your organization could take.

_____

_____

_____

_____

_____

_____

_____

6. Figure 5-3.1 depicts the formal educational system. Fill the ovals with ideas for the most important corporate actions that could positively influence the educational system and the education of an individual. (Extracurricular activities can be included in the approximate places where they would occur.) Possible ideas include summer jobs, learning about the corporation or industry, teaching aids, job fairs and comic books.

Figure 5-3.1. The Formal Educational System.

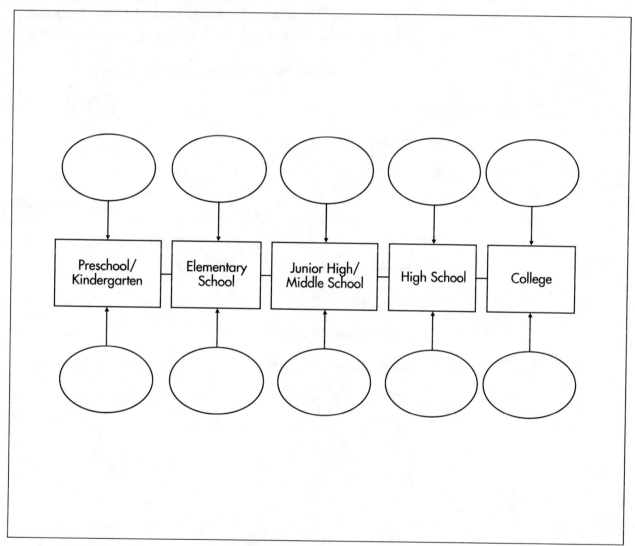

TREND 5-4 | The Requirements of the Emerging Global Society Are Diverging from the Knowledge Base of the U.S. Population

Increasing global integration requires workers to be more educated. Competition, complexity, and the knitting together of the world economies and cultures stresses the knowledge base of the U.S. work force.

1. Evaluate your workers' skills against the requirements of the emerging global society. Rate these skills on a scale of 1 to 5, with 5 highest in importance.

Our workers need improvement in:

Literacy   _____

Basic math skills   _____

Technological literacy   _____

Computer skills   _____

Basic sciences   _____

Geography/foreign cultures   _____

Foreign languages   _____

Ability to reason/draw conclusions   _____

Spatial and visual skills   _____

2. List the skills in exercise 1 in one of these two categories.

We train workers for the skill	*We hire workers with the skill*

TREND 5-5	Office Automation Thrives Despite Questionable Gains in Productivity

Office automation is a fact of life in most organizations. Resources are committed to its installation and upgrading, as well as to the necessary training to support it, although returns on such investments are not fully known.

1. Over the past ten years, what has the impact of office automation been on your organization? Circle your response.

positive   **negative**   **both**   **no impact**

How and where have the effects been felt?

2. Draw a time line on the following graph, showing the significance, over the next fifteen years, of office automation for your organization.

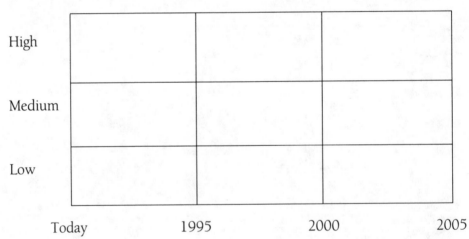

3. Identify tasks (blue-collar factory tasks or white-collar office tasks) in your organization that have recently been automated. Characterize any noticeable impact on productivity (gain, large gain, no change, loss, large loss).

Tasks Automated   *Productivity Gains*

_____   _____

_____   _____

_____   _____

_____   _____

_____   _____

_____   _____

4. Identify ways in which training could help workers adjust to the new tools of office automation.

_____

_____

_____

_____

_____

_____

_____

_____

5. Estimate as clearly as you can how many dollars are already spent on training per worker and equipment per worker in your organization. Is that gap significant?

6. List areas where automation could help alleviate the labor shortage.

_____

_____

_____

_____

_____

Artificial Intelligence Is Jerkily Moving from the Laboratory to Practical Application

Artificial intelligence (AI) has only just begun to enter the workplace. It brings with it a potential for profound change, with its ability to mimic functions that are especially well developed in humans or unique to the human mind (such as reading, speech, and judgment).

1. Using the following matrix, evaluate human resources impacts of potential roles for artificial intelligence in the workplace. Rate the impacts from 1 to 5, with 5 highest for the strength of the impact. You may wish to add categories on either axis. Indicate whether the impacts are positive (+) or negative (−).

Impacts

Potential Roles	Workers' attitudes	Worker's skills	Management practices	Job design	_____	_____
Expert systems generate speech						
Expert systems translate written language						
Expert systems recognize objects						
Expert systems replace people						
Expert systems teach people						
Expert systems manage and monitor						
Expert systems make decisions						
Expert systems make judgments						

2. List some positive steps that human resources can and should take, now and over the next decade, to smooth the way for increased use of artificial intelligence.

_____

_____

_____

_____

_____

_____

_____

3. What tasks, jobs, or activities in your organization could be most clearly assisted by artificial intelligence?

_____

_____

_____

_____

_____

_____

4. What activities in your organization are most difficult (if not impossible) to augment or replace with artificial intelligence? Describe specifically, for one or two of these jobs or tasks, why you think they cannot be replaced or enhanced by artificial intelligence.

_____

_____

_____

_____

_____

THEME 6

Rising Employee Expectations: Striking a Balance Between Demands and Costs

Workers and employers face steeply rising costs for health care. At the same time, the demand for health care and preventive care is rising. New and newly identified maladies contribute to the pressures.

Identify four or five recent issues that your organization has faced, where a demand for benefits had to be weighed against costs to the corporation.

_____

_____

_____

_____

_____

_____

The United States Is an Increasingly Sedentary Society

Workers' health and fitness are essential to performance, productivity, and morale. However, Americans are increasingly sedentary, and many are chronically unfit.

Some Data

Health Problems

- 19.2 million people have trouble walking a quarter-mile
- 12.8 million people have trouble reading, even with glasses
- 7.7 million people have trouble hearing conversations
- 2.5 million people have trouble making their speech understood
- Pain cost: 550 million lost workdays per year

Source: Data from "Health Problems." *The Wall Street Journal*, Mar. 18, 1987.

1. Score your organization's average worker. In your judgment, do 10 percent or more fall into any of the following categories?

   _____ Utterly fit and healthy

   _____ Committed to a program of exercise

   _____ Of average fitness and health

   _____ Utterly unfit for most routine tasks

   _____ Smokers

   _____ Excessive drinkers

2. Name some on-the-job incentives and reminders that could promote better
    fitness and health. Which would you personally prefer?

    _____   In-house health clinic

    _____   In-house fitness facilities

    _____   Regularly used stairways

    _____   Routine checkups

    _____   Corporate culture that emphasizes health and fitness

    _____   Good role models among staff

    _____   Other _____

                       _____

                       _____

                       _____

3. Consider your own child, or another child with whom you are familiar, and
    describe his or her health and wellness status as reliably as you can. What
    are the future implications of that child's being a worker? What could his or
    her parents, or the parents' employers, do to improve the child's health?
    Why bother?

| TREND 6-2 | Strong Long-Term Forces Work Against Cutting Health Costs |

Employers spend about 8 percent of their payroll budgets on health care. The costs are rising steadily and, it appears, unstoppably. ("Employee Benefits, 1988." *Medical Benefits*, Jan. 15, 1988, p. 4.)

1. Assess your organization's health programs. List the amenities for health care, preventive care, and workplace health and fitness already in place.

_____

_____

_____

_____

_____

_____

_____

2. List five programs your organization could (should) add or drop that would help fight the rising costs of health care.

_____

_____

_____

_____

_____

Discussion

How fit is your work force? What demands will your workers, collective fitness level place in your organization's health program in the future?

| TREND 6-3 | The Significance of the Worker's Contribution to Occupational Health and Safety Is Increasing |

Changing technology and new kinds of work have given rise to chronic workplace health problems. With automation, the worker must participate more in maintaining workplace health and safety.

Some Data

- In 1987, 11,100 workers died as a result of workplace accidents.
- In the same year, 1.8 million workers had disabling injuries.

Source: Data from U.S. Bureau of the Census. *Statistical Abstract of the United States, 1989.* Washington, D.C.: GPO, 1989, p. 413.

1. Review your experience with incidents involving on-the-job injury to workers. Were the accidents caused by employees' negligence, drug or alcohol problems, management practices, poorly designed processes and procedures, or faulty equipment?

Incident or Type of Incident	*Likely Cause(s)*
_____	_____
_____	_____
_____	_____
_____	_____
_____	_____

2. In the case of an employee-caused incident, which of the following factors may have contributed to the problem?

_____ Lack of skills/knowledge

_____ Life-style problems, substance abuse

_____ Physical condition

_____ Mental condition

_____ Fatigue

_____ Communication problems, including problems with language

_____ Morale problems

3. Of the factors listed in exercise 2, identify the most important ones for maintaining workers's health and safety.

_____

_____

_____

_____

_____

4. List some ways workers can be involved in trying to reduce the possibility of such incidents.

_____

_____

_____

_____

_____

_____

5. Considering yourself and the small number of workers whom you know best, what are the principal job- or occupation-related health concerns among you? What could you as a worker do? What could a manager do?

Discussion

To combat problems such as the ones discussed in the preceding exercises, what programs should your organization consider? What privacy issues could be involved in combating these problems?

TREND 6-4 | The AIDS Epidemic Is Killing People in the Prime of Their Working Lives

AIDS is a still-evolving social issue. As more and more organizations gain experience with workers who have AIDS, new practices and policies will emerge.

1. Do you have policies established for workers with AIDS?

2. Rate the possible impact of AIDS on your work force. Circle your response.

High   Medium   Low

How do you expect this situation to change over time?

3. Imagine that you have just received a positive HIV test result, indicating that you may be in a pre-AIDS condition. According to the most widely accepted current evidence, you may be dead within the next seven to nine years. Define, in the most plausible way, a humane program that could be established by your employer to assist you or work with you during that uncertain period.

Discussion

How is this issue evolving in your organization?

THEME 7

A Renewed Social Agenda: Expanding Corporate Social Responsibility

Such issues as workplace health and safety, environmental contamination, drug abuse, poor education, and the aftershocks of mergers and acquisitions put pressures on the employer to accept new social responsibilities.

In the following matrix, check off what you think the appropriate role of the organization is for each issue. List additional items that you believe are part of the social agenda increasingly facing the corporation.

_____

_____

_____

_____

_____

_____

_____

_____

Corporate Role

Issue	Pay for	Study	Design	Implement	Advise workers	Educate public	Stay out of	Avoid/ deny
Educational reforms								
Health care								
Business ethics								
Mergers and acquisitions								
Environmental problems								
Drug problems								
Child care								
Elder care								
Immigration policy								
Product safety								
U.S. competitiveness								
Affirmative action								
Pay equity								

| TREND 7-1 | Pent-Up Demand for Solutions to Workplace Issues Will Increase Regulation |

Workplace issues are increasingly answered with legislation for new regulation. The agenda of issues is constantly evolving as conditions, pressures, and regulatory solutions arise. Issues emerging today include the following:

- The erosion of employment-at-will policies
- Parental leave
- Family-support legislation
- Modifications to the Tax Reform Act of 1986
- Minimum-wage increases
- Mandatory health benefits
- Drug testing
- Polygraph testing
- Alien documentation
- Smoking in the workplace.

1. Consider one or more of the points just listed. Write what you would see as the ideal federal legislation in that area, striking an effective balance among personal, societal, and corporate considerations. Is your company now advocating such a position? Why? Why not?

2. Suppose that your organization were entitled to a seat in Congress. What would your representative pursue in new legislation, as an ideal agenda from your organization's perspective?

_____

_____

_____

_____

_____

_____

_____

3. Consider the same scenario for a corporate representative to your state legislature. What agenda would he or she bring to the legislature in representing the interests of the organization and its workers? What current trends in legislation would he or she fight against?

_____

_____

_____

_____

_____

_____

_____

TREND 7-2 | Corporations Are Under Pressure to Explore and Redefine Their Ethics

The rising interest in business ethics is due to recent financial scandals, effects of the rise in information technology, product safety, and other factors.

Use the future wheel in Figure 7-2.1 to analyze forces acting on your organization that may bring pressure to explore and redefine organizational ethics over the next ten or fifteen years. Some possible outside forces are listed here for you to consider. In adding your own, consider forces specific to your area of business, in addition to societywide issues.

Legislation   New technologies
Public attitudes   Scandals on Wall Street
The press   Whistleblowing

Figure 7-2.1. Future Wheel.

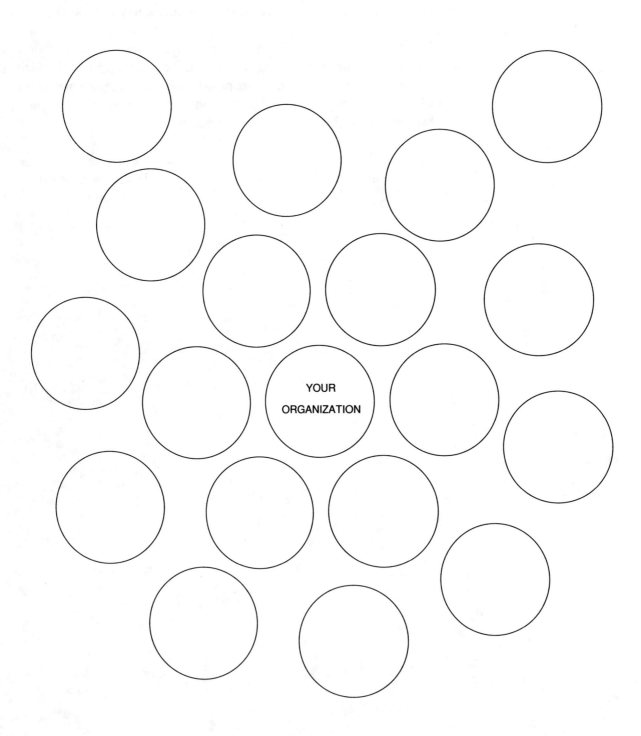

Discussion

Organizations could choose to treat ethical matters simply as questions of good business. Do you agree with this strategy? Why or why not? Consider a few specific issues in order to test your opinions.

Boards Are Stressed by Accountability, New Business Arrangements, and More Diverse Membership

Boards of directors are facing new pressures. Increasingly, they are besieged by new issues, are held accountable for outcomes, and face demands from both inside and outside the organization.

1. Fill the boardroom chairs in Figure 7-3.1 with the names of members of your organization's board of directors. Identify each member by gender, ethnic group, business background, and approximate age.

Figure 7-3.1. Your Board of Directors.

2. Is this board appropriate to your organization?

3. Under the stresses of new issues and accountability, whom do you want to see on your board? Why? (Examples are women, foreign nationals, scientists, former bureaucrats, minorities, lawyers, religious leaders, younger people, physicians, engineers, and social scientists.)

New Kinds of Members	*Reasons*
_____	_____
_____	_____
_____	_____
_____	_____
_____	_____
_____	_____

4. Fill the chairs in Figure 7-3.2 with your ideal board of directors.

Figure 7-3.2. Your Ideal Board of Directors.

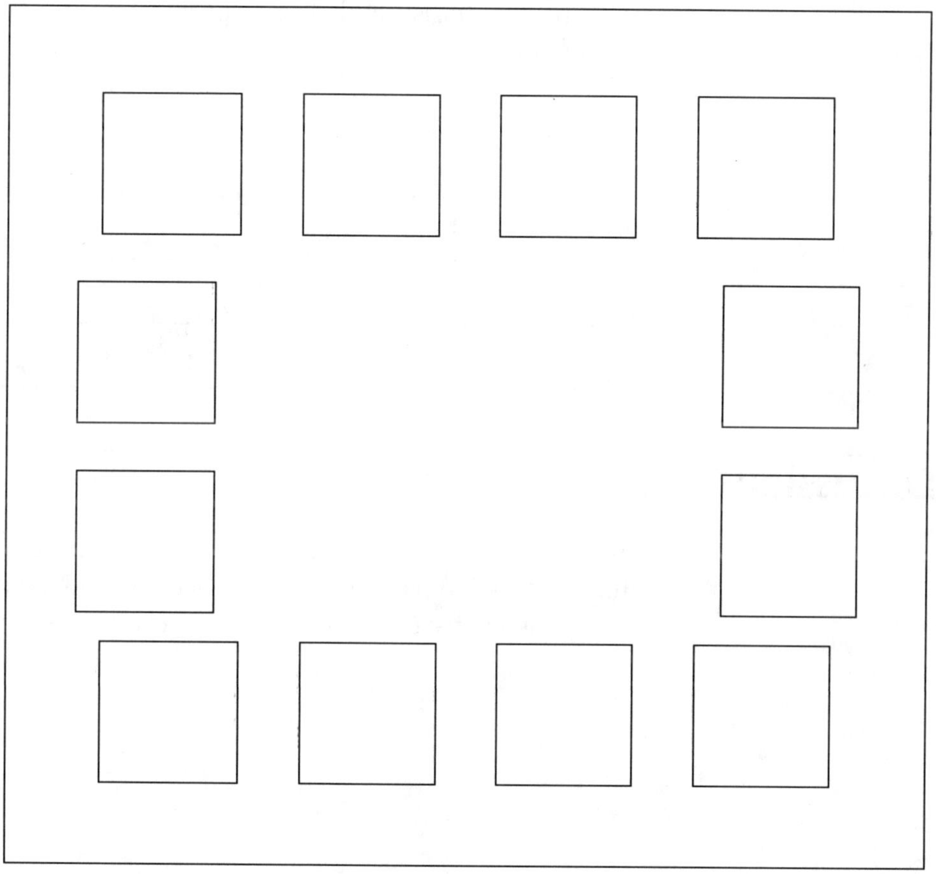

| Unions Innovate to Gain Members and Cope with a Changing Environment

Unions are changing with changes in business, the economy, and society. Many unions are losing members, while certain others are thriving. The survival and success of unions may depend on new forms of unions, new kinds of relationships with management, and unions' success with emerging workplace issues.

1. Imagine that you are an organizer for a labor union, attempting to unionize one of your facilities or the whole company. As specifically and straight-forwardly as possible, state several key issues that the union could promote.

_____

_____

_____

_____

_____

2. Imagine that your company has experienced a substantial business downturn. State the issues that could promote interest within your organization in unionizing.

_____

_____

_____

_____

_____

Discussion

What will the union of the future be like in your industry? Who will its members be? What will it seek to accomplish? How do the new issues and roles that you have identified fit in with your image of the union of the future?

PUTTING IT ALL TOGETHER

Imagine that it is the year 2005, and the coauthors of *The 100 Best Companies to Work for in America* have selected your company for inclusion. As completely as possible, describe what the first-class organization would be like.

EPILOGUE

The goal of this workbook is to broaden and deepen your thinking about a wide range of human resources issues for the future and about the impact of trends on the American work force. We hope that you will apply this new thought and learning from the workbook and from the book. We also encourage you to look past the exercises here and find out more about the emerging future of your organization.

DATE DUE

Printed
in USA

HIGHSMITH #45230